PURE
UNLIMITED
LOVE

D0126707

PURE

UNLIMITED

LOVE

AN ETERNAL

CREATIVE FORCE

AND BLESSING TAUGHT

BY ALL RELIGIONS

SIR JOHN TEMPLETON

TEMPLETON FOUNDATION PRESS
PHILADELPHIA & LONDON

Templeton Foundation Press
Five Radnor Corporate Center, Suite 120
100 Matsonford Road
Radnor, Pennsylvania 19087

© 2000 by Templeton Foundation Press

All rights reserved. No part of this book may be used or
reproduced, stored in a retrieval system, or transmitted in
any form or by any means, electronic, mechanical,
photocopying, recording, or otherwise, without the written
permission of Templeton Foundation Press.

Library of Congress Cataloging-in-Publication Data

Templeton, John, 1912-
Pure unlimited love / John Templeton.
p. cm.
Includes bibliographical references.
ISBN 1-890151-41-6 (alk. paper)
1. Love—Religious aspects—Christianity. I. Title.

BV4639 .T39 2000
291.5'677—dc21
00-029881

Designer and typesetter: Caroline Kulp Kline
Printer: McNaughton and Gunn, Inc., Saline, MI

Printed in the United States of America

00 01 02 03 04 05 06   10 9 8 7 6 5 4 3 2 1

PURE

UNLIMITED

LOVE

Unselfish Love

Unlimited love was called agape by the ancient Greeks to distinguish the divine love from earthly emotions. Unlimited love means total constant love for every person with no exception. The apostle John described unlimited love when he wrote, "*God is love and he who abides in love abides in God, and God abides in him*" (1 John 4:16 RSV).

God's unlimited love may be the basic reality from which all else is only fleeting perceptions by humans and other transient creatures. All the great religions have taught us how to love and worship. St. Paul wrote as translated in the New Jerusalem Bible, "*Love is always patient and kind; love is never jealous; love is not boastful or conceited, it is never rude and never seeks its own advantage, it does not take offense or store up grievances. Love does not rejoice at wrongdoing, but finds its joy in the truth. It is always ready to make allowances, to trust, to hope, and to endure whatever comes. Love never comes to an end*" (1 Corinthians 13:5-8).

Love seems to be the ideal and the dream, in some manner of expression, of every person. Could our souls have been conceived in the Creator's love and could it be that love foreshadows our destiny? We seem more fulfilled when we are in a state of *spiritual* love and, somehow, emptied when our focus moves elsewhere. Is it possible that love becomes the purpose of our existence? Although billions of words have been written about love in its many expressions, not one, or all, of them can fully capture the essence of love.

Sometimes when we think we love someone, we may be actually loving what we think the other person could give to us. This type of thinking can be an aspect of conditional or limited love. Love, at its highest and unlimited level, requires nothing in return. Unlimited love loves simply for the sake of loving. It doesn't seem concerned with *what* or *whom* it loves, nor with whether or not love is returned. Like the sun, its joy is manifest in the shining forth of its nature. Unlimited love can be considered a sacred power because it provides a positive and meaningful avenue through which we can relax the struggle between ourselves and others. Often, it is this struggle that lies at the root of human discord and suffering. Life has a wondrous natural sacredness that shines most brightly when we get our limited thinking and personal prejudices out of the way.[1]

Love Produces Peace

Scholars throughout the ages have defined love as the power that joins and binds the universe and everything in it; and love is often called the greatest harmonizing principle known to man. Teilhard de Chardin observed that love is the *"only force that can make things one without destroying them."* Love has the power to transform lives, to heal sickness, to mute evil, and to create harmony out of discord.

How do we identify unselfish, unlimited love? No one ever saw love, or heard love, or touched, smelled, or tasted love—literally. How can a person physically touch a thought, an idea? Certainly, we can *see* the effects of love, but not the divine energy creating the effects. We can *hear* the sound of compassion and caring in a voice. But how can we *taste* the sweetness of inner peace or spontaneous joy? We may *see* love in the actions of others as they express this innate energy from within themselves to serve another person. We may *smell* love through the dinner so lovingly prepared by one who loves to cook. We may *touch* love in the embraces of dear ones as they open up their hearts and let their love flow toward us. The five senses can sense only love from within, outward. Thus, as we express love, we are the first to receive love. We recognize in others that which we are. After all these words, love can best be described through experience, and then description becomes unnecessary!

Someone once said, "*When your heart is filled with love you will not be critical or irritable, but you will be divinely irresistible.*" Love is an inherent power that, if allowed to be expressed in one's life, can transform disharmony, heal disease, and transmute negative conditions into part of a harmonious whole. The results of love are always good. But do not confuse sentiment and sympathy with love. Our focus in this book is the purified, transcendent power of divine love that is expressed through our hearts and minds when we are open and receptive to it and when we recognize, understand, and encourage love in its unlimited capacity.

Whoever you are, whatever your background, at whatever point you may be in your spiritual journey, you are invited to discover a way of living that could possibly enhance every area of your life.

What is the Law of Unselfish, Unlimited Love?

In love, the ages of my soul spring open,
Allowing me to breathe a new air of freedom
And forget my own petty self.
In love, my whole being streams forth
Out of the rigid confines of
Narrowness and self-assertion,
Which make me a prisoner
Of my own poverty and emptiness.

—KARL RAHNER

LET US LOOK at some basic questions many
people have asked. Billions of stars shine

overhead in the night sky. Why? Several billion people live on our earth. What are we doing here? We think, feel, communicate, and exist. What is our purpose? What is humanity? What is our place in the universal scheme of things? Days, weeks, months, and years pass. Where are we going?

In view of the magnitude of these questions, how can a person find real purpose in life? Sometimes love gains great heights, seeing all things as originating from one universal source and, therefore, feels a sense of profound unity and kinship with them. From this viewpoint, love is intuitively perceived as a cosmic principle. In the words of Dante, it is: *"the love that moves the sun and all the stars."*[2]

Not until we comprehend and learn to work with the law of love and nonresistance does truth really become a *way of life*. As the apostle Paul says in his classic essay in First Corinthians 13:3, "*If with these things I have not love, I am nothing.*" Notice that Paul does not say that *in the absence of love* I have no real personality, no real influence, no existing life. He doesn't say that without love I am handicapped and may have a rough time. He says that "*without love, I am nothing!*" What could he mean by this statement? An Islamic Sufi text tells us: "*God looks not at your bodies or your forms, but He looks at your hearts.*"[3]

Unselfish, unlimited love accents the completeness of life. It is the ever-present potential through which we can find the fulfilling action or the harmonious attitude. In scripture, Jesus tells us to *"love one another"* (John 15:17). And he repeats the statement. Why? Although it is nice to love people, it is because the expression of love—unconditionally and with no limits or restrictions—radiates a great fundamental, invisible reality.

Through unlimited love a person can enter the dimension of spiritual unity and wholeness and maturity. Love is the fairest flower in God's garden. It has been referred to as *"the crowning grace of humanity, the holiest right of the soul, the golden link which binds us to duty and truth, the redeeming principle that chiefly reconciles the heart of life, and is prophetic of eternal good.*"[4] Mature love can become an avenue of spiritual influence that breaks down the walls that separate us from others. Mature spiritual love can unite us more closely with God and those around us. Surely our world will be a better place when the power of love replaces the love of power.

Benefits of Unlimited Love

Love is remembering to love the Lord,
our God, with all our hearts, with all
our souls, with all our minds, with all
our strength, and to love ourself . . . and
to love our neighbor as ourself.

LOVE SERVES. Love heals. Love reaches beyond imaginary boundaries between individuals, nations, and governments. Love can reach beyond self-interests to nurture benefits for strangers and make dreams and visions a reality.

A beginning step in love's outworking can

be learning how to control our emotional nature by keeping it constructively busy. In this way, we can begin to respect and appreciate the greater value of a loving nature. Living is part of the process of learning and growing in wisdom from life's experiences. One lesson worth learning early can be that life reflects back to us what we give to life. Among the greatest gifts we may offer to our world are love, joy, peace, patience, kindness, goodness, faithfulness, gentleness, and self-control. These are the gifts of a humble and sincere individual and spring directly from the heart.

"*The intellect by itself moves nothing,*" said Aristotle, and modern psychology seems to affirm this statement. We encounter those circumstances in life that reflect the quality of our deeper consciousness: thought and feeling, mind and heart, blended into our actions. When we exhibit those attributes in our lives, others benefit because these qualities have the effect of radiating like sunlight.

The universe is not isolated from us, nor are we from it! An old adage states, *"Rain falls on the just and the unjust."* Similarly, divine love expresses itself through all phases of creation. Surely, the foremost quality of divine nature could be all-encompassing love. Other qualities such as power, wisdom, grace, justice, and so on may be attributes of the Creator's caring for his creatures; but his love is preeminent—and unlimited.

God's love is given to us not because we deserve it. In fact, most likely when we need love the most is when we are the most unlovable. Worthiness is not a prerequisite to receive the benefit of God's love or grace. Those who are philosophically included may find it helpful to understand God's unlimited love as the original and ongoing basic creative force of the universe. This love was present before the beginning, and it continues to hold all things together. Our fleeting human emotions and perceptions are in fact mere glimpses of God's perfect love.

Embracing agape does not make us God, but the Bible suggests that, unlike other forms of love, it allows us in some way to participate in divinity.

WHY MUST UNLIMITED LOVE
BEGIN WITH ME?

*It is far more important that we learn
how to give love than to receive it. The
whole world could love us and we could
still be miserable. The great challenge is
not in getting love but in giving it. And
our spirit of giving originates within.*

WHENEVER OUR HEART opens to every
person, we experience a moment of divine,
unlimited love. People commonly imagine
that unlimited love represents a high or
distant ideal, one that may be difficult, if not

impossible, to obtain. Although unlimited love may be hard to put into everyday practice, its nature is quite simple and ordinary, which is humbly opening and responding to everyone without reservation.

We often glimpse the quality of unlimited love most vividly in beginnings and endings— at births, deaths, and when first falling in love. These are the times when we may be least under the influence of conditioned, habitual patterns of perception.

Something vast inside of us connects with something in others. A quality of great love is that it can either take hold of a situation or completely release it.

When our child is born, we do not consciously decide to love this infant. The freely flowing feeling of love is simply present. When someone close to us is dying, we often feel touched and present in ways that go beyond the fluctuations of the relationship. As reflected by this book's title, perfect love is pure in its essence and unlimited both in its scope and its degree. Perhaps pure, unlimited love is an ideal that can never be fully achieved in this life. Elusive though it may be, it is nevertheless a worthy goal for all to pursue.

To maintain an open heart does not mean we set aside all caution. And heaven need not be an image of some higher realm above and apart from this world. Rather, it indicates a way in which the human spirit is vast and open like the sky. Our reality can never be entirely encompassed by personality, the limitations of conditioning, or the constraints of form and matter. If neglecting earth is like having our heads in the clouds, neglecting heaven is like slogging through mud. If we refuse to let go of the old "stuff" and expand our boundaries beyond a need for control and security, we could lose a sense of greater vision or adventure.

Bringing the two sides of our nature together (the human and the divine) can be an ongoing, creative endeavor that continually moves us in new directions. If we neglect either the heights or depths of our experiences in life, we can only stagnate. When we bring the two together while attending to the practical details of everyday life, our love can gather power and momentum.

When we can love enough, we find a fulfillment and a true closeness to others that satisfies our desire to reach another person's heart. When we do not love enough to enter into this wholesome, freeing union with others, we tend to seek to solve our basic problem of separation by gaining power over others. We may tend to live by comparison. We may try to analyze how much better or more important we are than others. We may tend to be competitive rather than cooperative and creative and helpful.

What Are Some Present Misunderstandings About the Word "Love"?

This love force can be harnessed if we listen to our own hearts and minds and follow its laws of life that lead to a joyous existence.

PROBABLY NO OTHER word in our language has been given so many definitions or been written about in such depth in poetry, plays, novels, and philosophical and theological texts as "love." The Greeks developed several definitions of love. *Eros* is romantic love, the kind that puts butterflies in your stomach. *Storge* is the type of love that we feel for members of our family; it is sometimes referenced as the love of security. *Phileo*, or companionship, is the type of love we feel for our friends. Perhaps the most important love, however, is *agape*.

Agape is the unselfish love that gives of itself and expects nothing in return. It is the love that grows as you give it to others. Miraculously, the more agape you give, the more you have left to give. It is the love that great spiritual teachers such as Jesus, Buddha, Muhammad, Lao Tzu, Confucius, and others taught us to practice.

It is said that there is no power in the

universe greater than love, and no act more important than loving. Meher Baba commented to his listeners once, "*Love has to spring spontaneously from within. It is in no way amenable to any form of inner or outer force. Love and coercion can never go together; but though Love cannot be forced on anyone, It can be awakened in him through Love itself. Love is essentially self-communicative. Those who do not have It catch It from those who have It. True Love is unconquerable and irresistible, and It goes on gathering power and spreading Itself, until eventually It transforms everyone whom It touches.*"

Agape is the holy, unconditional love God gives us regardless of what we look like, how much money we have, how smart we are, and even regardless of how unloving our actions may sometimes be. When we practice agape, it becomes easier to love our enemies, to tolerate those who annoy us, and to find something to appreciate in every person we meet.

The great paradox of unlimited love is that it calls on us to be fully ourselves and honor our individual truth (the earth principle), while letting go of self-centeredness and giving without holding back (the heaven principle). Balance becomes necessary and important. Love in the fullest, richest way doesn't just fall into our lap like manna from heaven. It needs to be cultivated.

We can look for a moment at the differences between *holy love* and *human love*. Holy love is based upon the spiritual awareness of oneness and unity among all humankind, while human love seems to be focused on individualistic and personal needs and desires. Holy love responds with compassion in the face of unloving actions from others, while human love often reacts from a deficiency of affection. Holy love can take a compassionate initiative in relationships, while human love can be aggressive in reaching out to others. Holy love is unlimited and productive of patience, forgiveness, tolerance, giving and thanksgiving, and prayer. Holy love does not ask anything in relationships because it contains its own greatest reward.

What evidence supports the review of holy love versus human love? Become an observer in your world. Look around you. Note people's responses in communication, for example. Unfortunately the word "love" has been used indiscriminately to describe qualities of relationships that may not be expressive of love. We often think of love as an approval of one who is lovable and only as long as he or she remains lovable. John says, "*God is love, and he who abides in love abides in God, and God abides in him*" (John 4:16). In other words, to the extent that this divine activity is allowed to be active within us, we can become a portion of the divine heart of divinity.

Sometimes people say, "I love you," when,

in reality, they may actually mean, "I need you." This represents the human aspect of love. To claim love as a motive when a person's intent may actually be to fulfill his own needs does not seem representative of holy love. Genuine love does not take from another person; rather it gives always. Unlimited love encourages strength and freedom and empowers a person rather than fosters dependency or weakness.

Can Love Be an Eternal Universal Force More Potent than Gravity, Light, or Electromagnetism?

GOD HAS WOVEN a marvelous tapestry for the eyes of his creatures to behold. But in a sense, we may have lost a certain level of perception, a dimension of seeing, a sense of presence in the providential design of all that is. It is important to move beyond a narrow, restrictive point of view, to look beyond numbers, formulas, and models to behold the greater objective, the process, the phenomenon of the miracle of life, as part of a larger, more marvelous and mysterious whole. Albert Einstein was fond of contrasting his mathematics with his spiritual views of reality. He stated "*I want to know how God created this world. I want to know his thoughts, the rest are details.*"[5]

Einstein seems to view God as dressed in questions more than answers. Questions can be an invitation to greater awareness. They often point us toward areas of our experience that need attention. When we allow the question that is implicit in our difficulty to become explicit, we are inviting our awareness to enter the situation and guide us. From this perspective, we could ask the question: Are our human concepts of God too small? Are they too human-centered? If a tiny wave is a temporary manifestation of the ocean of which it is a part—does that resemble our relationship to God?

Because of the very nature of humanity, we find ourselves in a frustrating dilemma. As finite physical beings we can be filled with self-centered urges. On the other hand, while we may be limited, we may live as a part of spiritual infinity—*a presence*—that impels us to reach for the highest spiritual ideals. What is this spiritual infinity?

John Polkinghorne wrote, "*The most obvious sign of purpose is an artifact, a contrivance constructed to fulfill a particular role. It is not surprising that those who first seriously used the insights of modern science to look for indications of the will of a Creator behind the pattern of the physical world sought to do so in those terms.*"[6] Sir James Jeans said that the universe was beginning to look not like a great machine bur rather a great thought.[7] Certainly, there is no conclusive argument for design and purpose, but there are strong evidences of ultimate reality more fundamental than the cosmos. So, if there is a phenomenal universal force, for example, in gravity, in the light spectrum, or in electromagnetism, can there not also be a tremendous unknown, or non-researched, potency, or force, in unlimited love? With earthly information now doubling every three years, can our comprehension of some of these intangibles of spirit also be multiplied more than one hundredfold?

Can Love Reduce Mental and Spiritual Poisons Like Anger, Fear, and Resentment?

HATRED IS NOT conquered by hatred, but by love. This law of love was taught by the ancient Hindus and has through the ages been taught by many others, including Jesus, who said, "*Do not return evil for evil, but overcome evil with good.*" How easy it is when encountering such persons to resort to anger, to "return evil for evil." And yet our experience tells us that such a response, though it might make us feel better for a little while, does not address the root of the problem. In fact, all it may do is to make two hateful people out of one. According to the spiritual law cited above, the only divine response to hateful persons is to look beyond their hateful expressions in an effort to discover, understand, and heal the underlying injury. Hate heaped upon hate will serve only to escalate hatred. But love has the capacity to heal, and thus to overcome hatred.

Holy love does not parallel alongside emotions of anger, fear, or resentment. However, it can be a transmuting force for greater good. Love looks through a telescope; envy through a microscope. The sunlight of love can transform the germs of jealousy and hate. It is impossible to express love with a clenched fist. Could unlimited love be the central progressive activity of the spiritual life? If so, how?

As the quality of our love improves, we learn not only to love more, but we learn to love more wisely. Those elements of negative expression such as anger, hate, fear, resentment, and so on no longer find an abiding place in our consciousness. It is from giving love away that we gain it as a personal experience.

Why is service to others an important aspect of unlimited love? Kindness, care, and consideration toward others have often been described as love in action. Each day offers opportunities for anyone to contribute some act of kindness for another and to be caring, considerate, understanding, and supportive. The Golden Rule, *"for this is the law and the prophets,"* (Matthew 7:12 RSV) offers a pattern, or plan, that we can read and follow and build upon to bring all kinds of good things into our lives to share with others.

As Jesus stated, *"The measure you give will be the measure you get"* (Matthew 7:2). The unique combination of thoughts, feelings, and actions we extend in our daily living become the works that return to us as the harvest! The harvest can be slim pickings or it can be abundant; it can be reaping of weeds or flowers! Remember, what goes through us has its effect upon us and returns to us.

In accordance with this law of love, the arithmetic of love differs from the arithmetic of numbers. Love is not a quantity that gets used up and then is either gone forever or must somehow be replenished. Rather, love is a quality that, when exercised and practiced, grows and becomes stronger.

Have you ever noticed that some people seem to be happy no matter what may be taking place in their lives? There is buoyancy to their spirit and a sparkle to their personalities. A kind of glowing energy field seems to radiate from their faces, their words, and even the way they walk! What is the source of this inner radiance?

As with others, this spiritual law of love has been confirmed by collective human experience. People who practice agape become better at it as time goes by. They become kinder, more patient, more tolerant and sensitive. This does not mean that people in some service professions do not need an occasional break from the intense and sometimes depressing situations they face each day. As human beings, our physical and emotional energies are limited, and sometimes people need time away to recharge their spiritual batteries. But over the long haul, those who have committed themselves to a life of love grow stronger and more committed. Once a person is captivated by agape, there is no turning back. Mother Teresa was possibly a more loving person in the final weeks of her life than she was when she began her ministry to the poor, for she had behind her years of practice.

DOES LOVE ACT AS A HEALING AGENT IN EVERY AREA OF LIFE?

SOME HAVE ASKED, could it be that the visible and known areas of life are only small, temporary manifestations of reality? By definition, we exist at the center of a *visible* universe—that portion of the universe that we are able to see. It seems we may have glimmers of knowing within the horizons of unknowing. If it is true that "*there is no place where God is not,*" and if "*God is love,*" (1 John 4:15) then could there be any place where love is not?

Enjoy the healing process of returning to love. Someone once said, *"Love can penetrate to the depths of the one who has the faith and audacity to live in it!"* Love can move immediately to eliminate impatience, unkindness, envy, possessiveness, conceit, boastfulness, rudeness, and other elements of self-concerns. If a person is sincere about living in a consciousness of unlimited love, he could possibly be headed for a new way of living and a new selfhood.

Unlimited love automatically produces worship, thanksgiving, giving, forgiving, and joy. History reveals increasingly rapid progress by research in the concepts in cosmology, physics, biology, and other studies of God's creativity. Hopefully, increasing research also may reveal, better human concepts of the basic invisible reality called unlimited love.

Basic reality seems to be that the more you try to be like God by radiating unlimited love, the more you become flooded by waves of love from others and from God. How wonderful for the world it would be if we could begin to say whenever we meet or depart, *"God loves you, and I do too."*

CAN UNLIMITED LOVE
ELIMINATE CONFLICTS?

AGAPE DEMANDS THAT we give others the
freedom to return or not to return our love.
And because it is unlimited, it keeps on giving
even when love is not returned. When we love
in this way, we are loving as God loves.

In the consciousness of love, one is able to
ignore adversity, insults, loss, and injustice.
Often, when a person becomes more con-
scious of the activity of unlimited love in his
being, the desire for improvement becomes
joyously irresistible! When we decide to live in

a consciousness of unlimited love, we increasingly develop the habit of becoming a more loving person. An important element in learning to love more is learning to understand others. If we are having a difficult time in communicating with another person, one effective thing we can do is to seek to understand the other person's perspective of the situation. There are underlying reasons people act the way they do. When we lovingly seek to understand another person, we increase the quality of communication—and that can open a seemingly stuck door.

"*The heart is the place of intelligence, understanding, and every positive human quality.*"[8] The more we give our thoughts and feelings to love, the more aware we can become of this great power within us. The soul may be inspired to move toward greater expressions of harmony, cooperation, and freedom. A fresh breeze blows through the corridors of the mind and heart and fans the emerging spark of peace and goodwill.

How Can Unlimited Love Assist a Person in Taking Responsibility?

Leo Buscaglia expressed beautifully the role of responsibility in love: "*When love is truly responsible, it is one's duty to love all [people]. [A person has] no choice but to accept this duty, for when he does not, he finds his alternatives lie in loneliness, destruction, and despair. To assume this responsibility is for him to become involved in delight in mystery and growth. It is to dedicate himself to the process of helping others to realize their love through him.*

Simply speaking, to be responsible in love is to help other [people] to love. To be helped toward realizing your love is to be loved by other [people].

"[People] have been known to approach this responsibility to love from different means, but the ends are always the same, universal love. Some begin with a deep personal involvement with another individual. From this, they learn that love cannot be exclusive. They learn that if love is to grow, it will need diverse minds, innumerable individuals, and the exploration of varied paths. No one human being can afford him all of these things, so he must enlarge his love to include all of mankind in his love. The more all-encompassing his love, the greater his

growth. The love of humanity is the natural outgrowth of love for a single individual. From one [person] to all [people]."[9]

How Can Unlimited Love be Helpful in Creating a Sacred Vision for You and Others?

How can we learn to be helpers in God's purposes? Along with the gift of individuality that God has so generously provided for each of us, he has also given us the priceless gift of personal free will. Why has God given us such a power? And, having the right of self-determination, what shall we do with ourselves and with this power? Perhaps a key response to the question lies in realizing God has a superb purpose for our lives. Possibly, are we created to become helpers in God's accelerating creativity?

In the Gospel of Mark 4:26–28, we find an example of God's creative Spirit at work: "*The kingdom of God [Love] is as if a man should scatter seed upon the ground, and should sleep and rise night and day, and the seed should sprout and grow, he knows not how. The earth produces of itself. First the blade, then the ear, then the full grain in the ear.*"

As we continue to contemplate and experience the creative spirit of unlimited love, we may feel a deep inner desire to attune more fully with God's will for the universe and its inhabitants. You may even find yourself prayerfully asking, "*Infinite Spirit of Love, what is your will for me and my world?*" And the still, small voice of Spirit may respond: "*Precious One, will you direct your blessings of love to go before you, like a messenger straight from the heart of God, to make your way peaceful, happy, and successful?*"

How May We Learn to Love Better?

REMEMBER AN IMPORTANT truth: whatever the need or circumstance, love can find a way to adjust, heal, or resolve any problem or situation.

When we invite unlimited love to serve as the backdrop for our lives, our world is intrinsically improved. It has been said that loving relationships with all of life are the radiant jewels in the crown of spiritual achievement! The spirit of unlimited love, which you build during your lifetime, may be that part of you which is immortal! Radiant unlimited love, universal—eternal!

Notes

1. John Marks Templeton, ed., *Worldwide Laws of Life: 200 Eternal Spiritual Principles* (Philadelphia: Templeton Foundation Press, 1997), p. 5.

2. Dante Alighieri, Divina Commedia, "Paradisco," 33,145.

3. William C. Chittick, trans., *Faith and Practice of Islam: Three Thirteenth Century Sufi Texts* (Albany, N.Y.: State University of New York Press, 1992), p. 240.

4. Unity Pamphlet: *Divine Love Works Through You*, Unity School of Christianity, Unity Village, Missouri, 1981.

5. Timothy Ferris, "The Other Einstein," *Science 83* (October 1982): p. 25–26.

6. John Marks Templeton, ed., *Evidence of Purpose* (Philadelphia, Pa.: Templeton Foundation Press, 1994), p. 105.

7. Ibid, p. 7.

8. Chittick, *Faith and Practice of Islam,* p. 6.

9. Leo Buscaglia, *Love* (New York: Ballentine Books, 1972), p. 158–159.